W9-CAU-582

Early American Wisdom

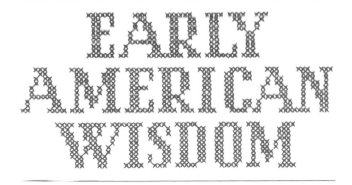

EARLY AMERICAN WISDOM

Good Thoughts From Yesterday
To Think About Today

Selected by Barbara Wells Price
Illustrated With Stitchery
By Susan Tinker

HALLMARK EDITIONS

*He who receives ideas from me, receives in-
struction himself without lessening mine; as
he who lights his taper at mine receives light
without darkening me.*

Thomas Jefferson

[A] master, being forced to sell a pair of his oxen to pay his servant his wages, told his servant he could keep him no longer, not knowing how to pay him the next year. The servant answered, he would serve him for more of his cattle. "But how shall I do," saith the master, "when all my cattle are gone?" The servant replied, "You shall then serve me, and so you may have your cattle again."

John Winthrop

Nature is the most thrifty thing in the world; she never wastes anything; she undergoes change, but . . . the essence re - mains....

Horace Binney

I have ever deemed it more honorable and more profitable, too, to set a good example than to follow a bad one.

Thomas Jefferson

I have not seldom blushed at their [Indians'] accounts of the treatment they have experienced from white men: but, I trust, the period is not far distant, when, for our own sakes, as well as for theirs, we shall endeavor to diffuse political security and happiness to the Indian nations with whom we have any intercourse; and to convert them into free men....

Jonathan Boucher

Ask council always of the wise,
    give ear unto the end,
And ne'er refuse the sweet rebuke
    of him that is thy friend.

The New England Primer

The glow of one warm thought is to me worth more than money.

Thomas Jefferson

I have but one lamp by which my feet are guided, and that is the lamp of experience. I know of no way of judging of the future but by the past. *Patrick Henry*

When the well is dry, we know the wealth of water.

Benjamin Franklin

I believe in the equality of man; and I believe that religious duties consist in doing justice, loving mercy, and endeavoring to make our fellow creatures happy.

Thomas Paine

Good humor is one of the preservatives of our peace and tranquility.

Thomas Jefferson

I must study politics and war that my sons may have liberty to study mathematics and philosophy. My sons ought to study mathematics and philosophy, geography, natural history and naval architecture, navigation, commerce and agriculture, in order to give their children a right to study painting, poetry, music, architecture....

John Adams

The end of all good government is to cultivate humanity and promote the happiness of all, and the good of every man in all his rights, his life, liberty, estate, honor, etc., without injury or abuse done to any.

John Wise

A little flattery will support a man through great fatigue.   *James Monroe*

The happiness of the domestic fireside is the first boon of mankind....

Thomas Jefferson

The capacity of the female mind for studies of the highest order cannot be doubted, having been sufficiently illustrated by its works of genius, of erudition, and of science....It merits an improved system of education.

James Madison

[There was once a] man who, in buying an ax of a smith...desired to have the whole of its surface as bright as the edge. The smith consented to grind it bright for him if he would turn the wheel; he turn'd, while the smith press'd the broad face of the ax hard and heavily on the stone, which made the turning of it very fatiguing. The man came every now and then from the wheel to see how the work went on, and at length would take his ax as it was, without farther grinding. "No," said the smith, "turn on, turn on; we shall have it bright by-and-by; as yet, it is only speckled." "Yes," says the man, "but I like a speckled ax best."

Benjamin Franklin

If thou thinkest twice, before thou speakest once, thou wilt speak twice the better for it.   *William Penn*

In affairs of love a young heart is never in more danger than when attempted by a handsome young soldier. A man naturally ordinary, when arrayed in a military habit, will make a tolerable appearance; but when beauty of person, elegance of manner, and an easy method of paying compliments, are united to the scarlet coat, smart cockade, and military sash, ah! well a day for the poor girl who gazes on him: she is in imminent danger; but if she listens to him with pleasure, 'tis all over with her, and from that moment she has neither eyes nor ears for any other object.

Susanna Haswell Rowson

Every government degenerates when trusted to the rulers of the people alone. The people themselves, therefore, are its only safe depositories.

Thomas Jefferson

We often repent of what we have said, but never, never, of that which we have not.

Thomas Jefferson

He is an American, who, leaving behind him all his ancient prejudices and manners, receives new ones from the new mode of life he has embraced, the new government he obeys, and the new rank he holds. He becomes an American by being received in the broad lap of our great *Alma Mater*. Here individuals of all nations are melted into a new race of men, whose labours and posterity will one day cause great changes in the world.

St. John de Crèvecoeur

When the heart has will the hands can soon find means to execute a good action.

Susanna Haswell Rowson

Associate with men of good quality, if you esteem your own reputation; for it is better to be alone than in bad company.

George Washington

Never buy what you do not want, because it is cheap; it will be dear to you.

Thomas Jefferson

Let us tenderly and kindly cherish...the means of knowledge. Let us dare to read, think, speak and write.

John Adams

History, by apprising [people] of the past, will enable them to judge of the future; it will avail them of the experience of other times and other nations; it will qualify them as judges of the actions and designs of men; it will enable them to know ambition under every disguise it may assume; and knowing it, to defeat its views.

Thomas Jefferson

Dost thou love life? Then do not squander time, for that is the stuff life is made of.

Benjamin Franklin

A ship that bears much sail, and little or no ballast, is easily overset; and that man whose head hath great abilities, and his heart little or no grace, is in danger of foundering.

Anne Bradstreet

...Were it left to me to decide whether we should have a government without newspapers, or newspapers without a government, I should not hesitate a moment to prefer the latter. *Thomas Jefferson*

Justice is the end of government. It is the end of society. *James Madison*

All nations of men have the same natural dignity, and we all know that very bright talents may be lodg'd under a very dark skin. The principal difference between one people and another proceeds only from the different opportunities of improvement. *William Byrd*

Make haste slowly.

Benjamin Franklin

TALL
OAKS
FROM
LITTLE
ACORNS
GROW

ON FAD-CONSCIOUS WOMEN

To speak moderately, I truly confess it is beyond the ken of my understanding to conceive how those women should have any true grace or valuable virtue that have so little wit as to disfigure themselves with such exotic garbs as not only dismantles their native lovely lustre but transclouts them into gant bar-geese, ill-shapen, shotten shellfish, Egyptian hieroglyphics, or at the best into French flirts of the pastry, which a proper English-woman should scorn with her heels; it is no marvel they wear drails on the hinder part of their heads, having nothing as it seems in the fore part but a few squirrels' brains to help them frisk from one ill-favored fashion to another.   *Nathaniel Ward*

Content makes poor men rich; discontent makes rich men poor.   *Benjamin Franklin*

True friendship is a plant of slow growth and must undergo and withstand the shocks of adversity before it is entitled to the appellation. *George Washington*

Error is always more busy than truth.

Hosea Ballou

No person will have occasion to complain of the want of time who never loses any.

Thomas Jefferson

...Swift time rolls, and on his rapid wheel bears the winged hours, and the circling years. *Mercy Otis Warren*

I think every nation has a right to establish that form of government, under which it conceives it may live most happy; provided it infracts no right, or is not dangerous to others; and that no governments ought to interfere with the internal concerns of another, except for the security of what is due to themselves.

George Washington

The world is my country,
All mankind are my brethren,
To do good is my religion,
I believe in one God and no more.

Thomas Paine

A little neglect may breed mischief: for want of a nail the shoe was lost; for want of a shoe the horse was lost; and for want of a horse the rider was lost.

Benjamin Franklin

...All great and honorable actions are accompanied with great difficulties and must be both enterprised and overcome with answerable courages.

William Bradford

Honesty
is the best
policy.

Benjamin Franklin

The time to guard against corruption and tyranny is before they shall have gotten hold of us. It is better to keep the wolf out of the fold than to trust to drawing his teeth and talons after he shall have entered.

Thomas Jefferson

I desire you would remember the ladies and be more generous and favorable to them than your ancestors. Do not put such unlimited power into the hands of the husbands. Remember, all men would be tyrants if they could. If particular care and attention is not paid to the ladies, we are determined to foment a rebellion, and will not hold ourselves bound by any laws in which we have no voice or representation....Men of sense in all ages abhor those customs which treat us only as the vassals of your sex; regard us then as being placed by Providence under your protection, and in imitation of the Supreme Being make use of that power only for our happiness.   *Abigail Adams*
(From a letter to her husband as the Constitution was being drawn up.)

He that falls in love with himself will have no rivals.   *Benjamin Franklin*

No great advance has ever been made in science, politics, or religion, without controversy.

Lyman Beecher

DARBY AND JOAN

When Darby saw the setting sun
   He swung his scythe, and home he run,
Sat down, drank off his quart, and said,
   "My work is done, I'll go to bed."
"My work is done!" retorted Joan,
   "My work is done! Your constant tone,
But hapless woman ne'er can say,
   'My work is done' till judgment day."

John Honeywood

I am mortified to be told that, in the United States of America, the sale of a book can become a subject of inquiry, and of criminal inquiry, too.

Thomas Jefferson

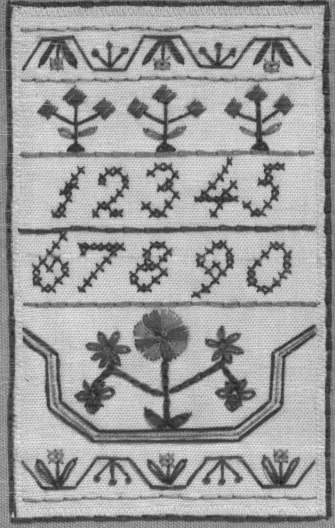

...A fond Mother never knows where to stop when her children is the subject.

Martha Jefferson Randolph

...When young I entertained some thoughts of selling my farm. I thought it afforded but a dull repetition of the same labours and pleasures. I thought the former tedious and heavy, the latter few and insipid; but when I came to consider myself as divested of my farm, I then found the world so wide, and every place so full, that I began to fear lest there would be no room for me.   *St. John de Crèvecoeur*

Suspicion is far more apt to be wrong than right; oftener unjust than just. It is no friend to virtue, and always an enemy to happiness.

Hosea Ballou

Trut
its d
its o

...in this world nothing is certain but death and taxes. *Benjamin Franklin*

...Infinite Love where'er we turn our eyes
Appears: this ev'ry creature's
    wants supplies;
This most is heard in Nature's
    constant voice,
This makes the morn,
    and this the eve rejoice;
This bids the fost'ring rains
    and dews descend
To nourish all,
    to serve one gen'ral end,
The good of man.... *Phillis Wheatley*

Good and evil I see is to be found in all societies, and it is in vain to seek for any spot where those ingredients are not mixed. *St. John de Crèvecoeur*

…Labor to keep alive in your breast that little spark of celestial fire, called Conscience.

George Washington

Wish not so much to live long as to live well.

Benjamin Franklin

Resolved, never to do anything which I should be afraid to do if it were the last hour of my life.

Jonathan Edwards

Honesty, sincerity, and openness I esteem essential marks of a good mind.

John Adams

A CURE FOR STEALING

In an hard and long winter, when *wood* was very scarce at *Boston*, a man gave him [John Winthrop] a private information that a needy person in the neighbourhood stole *wood* sometimes from *his* pile; whereupon the governour in a seeming anger did reply, "Does he so? I'll take a course with him; go, call that man to me; I'll warrant you I'll cure him of stealing." When the man came, the governour considering that if he had *stolen* it was more out of *necessity* than *disposition*, said unto him, "Friend, it is a severe winter, and I doubt you are but meanly provided for wood; wherefore I would have you supply your self at my wood-pile till this cold season be over." And he then merrily asked his friends, "Whether he had not effectually cured this man of stealing his wood?"

Cotton Mather

WASHINGTON'S PRAYER FOR THE UNITED STATES

Almighty God; we make our earnest prayer that Thou wilt keep the United States in Thy holy protection; that Thou wilt incline the hearts of the citizens to cultivate a spirit of subordination and obedience to government...and finally that Thou wilt most graciously be pleased to dispose us all to do justice, to love mercy and to demean ourselves with that charity, humility and pacific temper of mind which were the characteristics of the Divine Author of our blessed religion, and without a humble imitation of whose example in these things we can never hope to be a happy nation. *George Washington*

Experience keeps a dear school, but fools will learn in no other.

Benjamin Franklin

The noblest mortal, in his entrance onto the stage of life, is not distinguished by any pomp or of passage from the lowest of mankind; and our life hastens to the same general mark: death observes no ceremony, but knocks as loud at the barriers of the Court as at the door of the cottage.   *John Wise*

Honesty is the first chapter in the book of wisdom.   *Thomas Jefferson*

Never leave that till tomorrow which you can do today.   *Benjamin Franklin*

There are two rules whereby we are to walk, one towards another: justice and mercy.

John Winthrop

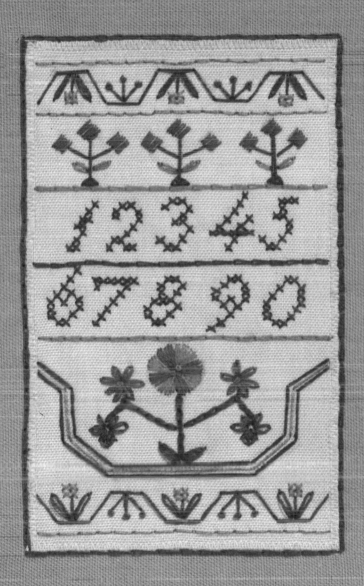

...A fond Mother never knows where to stop when her children is the subject.

Martha Jefferson Randolph

...When young I entertained some thoughts of selling my farm. I thought it afforded but a dull repetition of the same labours and pleasures. I thought the former tedious and heavy, the latter few and insipid; but when I came to consider myself as divested of my farm, I then found the world so wide, and every place so full, that I began to fear lest there would be no room for me.   *St. John de Crèvecoeur*

Suspicion is far more apt to be wrong than right; oftener unjust than just. It is no friend to virtue, and always an enemy to happiness.

Hosea Ballou

Truth often suffers more by the heat of its defenders, than from the arguments of its opposers.

William Penn

When angry, count ten before you speak; if very angry, an hundred.

Thomas Jefferson

So very pliable a thing is frail man, when women have the bending of him.

William Byrd

There are two sorts of people in the world, who with equal degrees of health, and wealth, and the other comforts of life, become, the one happy, and the other miserable. This arises very much from the different views in which they consider things, persons, and events; and the effect of those different views upon their own minds

Benjamin Franklin

Conduct is more convincing than language....

John Woolman

We cannot act with too much caution in our disputes. Anger produces anger; and differences that might be accommodated by kind and respectful behaviour, may by imprudence be changed to an incurable rage.

John Dickinson

No man should part with his own individuality and become that of another.

William Ellery Channing

Therefore, let us choose life, that we, and our seed, may live....

John Winthrop

We hold these truths to be self-evident: That all men are created equal; that they are endowed by their Creator with certain inalienable rights; that among these are life, liberty, and the pursuit of happiness.

Thomas Jefferson

For my own part, I never did, nor do I believe I ever shall, give advice to a woman, who is setting out on a matrimonial voyage; first, because I never could advise one to marry without her own consent; and, secondly, because I know it is to no purpose to advise her to refrain, when she has obtained it. *George Washington*

These are the times that try men's souls.

Thomas Paine

...I am determined to be cheerful and happy in whatever situation I may be. For I have also learned from experience that the greater part of our happiness, or misery depends on our dispositions and not on our circumstances. We carry the seeds of the one or the other about with us in our minds wherever we go.

Martha Washington

INDEX

Set in Janson, a distinguished seventeenth-century
Old Style face issued by Anton Janson,
a Leipzig typefounder, between 1660 and 1687.
Printed on Hallmark Eggshell Book paper.
Designed by Bruce Baker.